Prayer
of
Quiet

Donna Fasano

Copyright © 2014 by Donna J. Fasano

ISBN Paperback: 978-1-939000-24-8
ISBN Large Print Paperback: 978-1-939000-22-4
ISBN eBook: 978-1-939-000-23-1

All rights reserved. The reproduction or utilization of this work, in whole or in part, in any form is forbidden without written permission from the copyright holder.

Printed in the USA

Locate the author:
On line: DonnaFasano.com
On Facebook: Facebook.com/DonnaFasanoAuthor
On Twitter: Twitter.com/DonnaFaz

Faith sees the invisible,
believes the unbelievable,
and receives the impossible.
~ Corrie ten Boom

God calls and you do not hear,
for you are preoccupied with your own voice.
~A Course in Miracles

As a child, I was taught by my parents, religious teachers, and youth group counselors that God is with us always, that God sees all, that God knows all. This knowledge—most fearful to a precocious child such as myself—kept me out of trouble and 'on the straight and narrow' for years. However, during my late teens and throughout my twenties I somehow lost sight of the concept of an ever-present God. As a young wife and devoted mother in ardent pursuit of a writing career, I allowed my spiritual development to go, well, undeveloped. Oh, I attended church regularly all throughout those years. I read my Bible. I prayed for myself, my family, and my friends. I even taught Sunday school for nearly twenty years. But I slowly came to the realization that, even in the midst of all that church participation, there was a gnawing emptiness inside me. I finally reached the conclusion that what was missing in my spiritual life was a truly intimate relationship with God.

    For the past thirty years I have committed myself to seeking and experimenting, all in a single-minded effort to find my beloved Creator—and I believe I have.

    God is not in some far away place called heaven, witnessing my every thought, word, and deed, all while keeping meticulous notes in the Book of Life on my spiritual successes and missteps. God is, and always has been, right with me. Just as God is, and always has been, right with you.

My father, an uncomplicated yet wise man, told me long ago that when babies are born a small piece of God is implanted in them. He didn't know how this happened. There are some things, he reasoned, that simply aren't meant to be understood. However, he believed it was so. At the time, he had been attempting to explain the human conscience in order to assuage his young daughter's curiosity regarding how people discern right from wrong. "Listen to your heart," he told me, "and God will help you understand if what you want to do is right or wrong." After all my spiritual searching, I have decided my father's elementary explanation holds more truth than either of us realized at the time.

I have always enjoyed a rich prayer life. If I or anyone I knew was in need, I would petition

God. If a loved one became ill, I would pray for healing. Whenever I experienced a wonderful event, I would get down on my knees and send my gratitude heavenward. I prayed before meals. I prayed at bedtime. I talked to God daily—and that's exactly what I did. *I talked to God.* I never imagined that God might have something to say to me. Quieting my voice, the audible one along with that pesky inner one, and *listening* never dawned on me. That is, until I read about The Prayer of Quiet.

    A prayer that offers the soul an extraordinary peace and rest? A prayer that brings the delight of contemplating God as truly present? A prayer that allows the practice of complete and total faith that God is available? A prayer that provides the attentive silence in which God can do the communicating?

    Yes, yes, yes, and *yes!* The Prayer of Quiet

is all these things and more.

This prayer isn't a new discovery. It is mentioned in the writings of Saint Francis of Assisi (1181-1226), Saint Teresa of Avila (1515-1582), and John of the Cross (1542-1591). Others have written about contemplative prayer, I'm sure, even contemporary authors. It is called silent prayer, holy reflection, prayer of the heart, and other names. However, neither the information nor the technique is much talked about or known. At least, not in my circles, and I didn't happen upon it until I was nearly fifty years old. This book is my small attempt to let others know about this method of prayer so more of God's children can begin a practice that is both spiritually constructive and completely life-altering.

Making yourself wholly available to God is a joyous experience. This simple prayer is an appropriate practice for people of all ages, adults and children alike. How I wish I had taught my children to spend silent time with God each and every day! Luckily, it is never too late to begin a habit that will surely enrich your life.

I suggest you begin slowly. Quieting your mind isn't an easy task, but as Saint Teresa wrote in The Interior Castle, "He who reasons less and tries to do least, does most in spiritual matters."

Earnestly opening your heart and mind to God for even one minute daily will be beneficial; then gradually increase your Quiet Prayer time to five minutes, which I'm sure will grow to ten, and then twenty. Imagine how twenty minutes each day spent in silent devotion will deepen your relationship with God. The quiet respite offered during the actual practice isn't the only blessing you'll receive from this prayer. The effects will carry over into your daily life in various and surprising ways. You will find yourself more awake to—*more aware of*—how the spiritual realm is working in every aspect of your day-to-day life, workings you were blind to before developing this spiritual practice.

    May you find a deep and profound solace in The Prayer of Quiet. I know I have.

It may be that one of our great faults in prayer is that we talk too much and listen too little. When prayer is at its highest, we wait in silence for God's voice; we linger in His presence for His peace and His power to flow over us and around us; we lean back in His everlasting arms and feel the serenity of perfect security in Him.

~William Barclay

Blessed are the pure of heart,
for they shall see God.
~Matthew 5:8

Choose

    Select a sacred word or phrase to be used during your prayer time. A simple, one syllable word is best. I suggest love, or peace, or rest, or Lord. Better yet, pray about it. I'm sure the perfect word will come to you. Your sacred word is not a mantra that is chanted over and over. It is simply a gentle reminder of your intent to commune with God should your attention wander. Calming the mind is difficult. If you find your thoughts go astray, simply use your sacred word to center yourself and return to that holy place within.

Relax

Sit in a comfortable position with your spine vertically straight. Falling asleep is not the objective. Sitting in a chair is perfectly acceptable, feet flat on the floor, palms facing either up or down on your thighs, whichever feels more natural. If you'd rather sit cross-legged on the floor, that will work too. Dip your chin slightly and imagine there is a string gently drawing your spine upward. Take five to ten slow, deep breaths, and consciously release all the pent-up tension in your shoulders. You may close your eyes or leave them open.

Release

Let go of all expectations and pre-conceived notions. This is a time to offer God your undivided attention, to be fully receptive—to wait in wonder.

Consent

    Give consent to God's presence. Words aren't necessary. Simply extend your permission with an intention that is pure. God is already with you, already available. Draw deeply on faith. Think of offering consent as stepping into a beam of warm, bright light. The light is waiting for you, has been waiting for you. All you have to do is move into it.

Breathe

Just be.
Still and serene.

Return

    Whenever an errant thought causes your attention to wander, don't fret. This is normal. Simply return to your sacred word; gently repeat your word, either out loud or silently, as a reminder of your intent. A loving objective to spend time listening to God is all that is needed.

Rest

Bask in the peace and tranquility
of abiding with God.

Afterthoughts

Communing with God is experiential and intimate. For one person to attempt to suggest what another might encounter during prayer practice is difficult, if not impossible, as God touches each beloved child in a different and unique way. In my personal practice, I have had a wide variety of experiences that include profound peace, deep contentment, elation, tingling of forearms, hands, legs, or feet, slight disorientation, a feeling of lightness or dizziness, visions of rolling color and flashes of light. Other experiences are too personal to even attempt to explain, but the most powerful and profound involved feeling loved in a way I can only express as both overwhelming and unearthly. There simply is not an emotion or a sensation on this corporeal plane that can compare to the warm, live, liquid Love that drenched my being and left me tearful, overwrought, and feeling utterly cherished. Unfortunately, these words are a puny description of how I felt.

Some might shy away from an aspect of The Prayer of Quiet that could be classified as mystical or New Age, but I would like to point out that many people mentioned in the Bible faced the mysterious, witnessed the supernatural. Ordinary people—just like you and me—experienced miracles; various people heard the voice of God or were visited by angels, a sea was parted, entire cities were destroyed, the sick and lame were healed, demons were exorcised, the dead were brought back to life, to name just a few. We are as much God's children as the people of the Bible. Why shouldn't we experience the miraculous?

There was a time when I did not feel worthy to seek direct communion with God, and there's a good chance you feel the same. We are told by our pastors, our priests, even the Bible itself, that we are guilty sinners. "For all have sinned, and come short of the glory of God" (Romans 3:23, KJV). Don't let that keep you from seeking your Creator.

God is omnipresent (present everywhere), omnipotent (all-powerful), and omniscient (all-knowing). God is also merciful. Most important of all, God is Love. It isn't difficult to understand that God's love is far more powerful than our sin. So seek the kingdom of God ardently, and the place in which to seek is inside yourself, for that is where Jesus himself told us the kingdom is located (Luke 17:21).

Whatever you sense or see or feel, whether

you reach a simple state of quiet restfulness or you "see visions" and "dream dreams" (Joel 2:28, KJV), I have no doubt you will find that practicing The Prayer of Quiet will transform you.

 May God bless you on your spiritual journey.

Recommended Reading

Some Christians might be reluctant to read holy texts from other religions or books featuring doctrine or spiritual philosophy that is different from their own personal practices. However, understanding the basic beliefs of your brothers and sisters across the globe will help you in two ways. Firstly, you will be less likely to feel distressed by the preaching or hate-speech of fanatics of any sort (because *"the truth will set you free"*). Secondly, learning that love, compassion, kindness, and ethical behavior is the basis of every religion will help you develop trust in your fellow human beings which will make you more able to follow the Bible's "love one another" edict. With these thoughts in mind, I offer you my Recommended Reading List:

The King James Bible/Amplified Bible, Parallel Edition
A Course In Miracles, Combined Edition
The Gnostic Gospels
Dhammapada
Bhagavad Gita
The Qur'an
Tibetan Book of The Dead
Tao Te Ching by Lao Tzu
How To Practice by The Dalai Lama
The Art of Happiness by The Dalai Lama
God is a Verb by Rabbi David A. Cooper
The Rhythm of Life by Matthew Kelly
The Sacred Art of Lovingkindness by Rabbi Rami Shapiro
Stillness Speaks by Eckhart Tolle
The Power of Now by Eckhart Tolle
The Seat of the Soul by Gary Zukav
The Four Agreements by Don Miguel Ruiz
Peace in Every Step by Thich Hnat Hanh
The Interior Castle by St. Teresa of Avila
Dark Night of the Soul by St. John of the Cross

Centering Prayer and Inner Awakening by Cynthia Bourgeault
Intimacy with God by Thomas Keating
The Spiritual Teaching of Ramana Maharshi
Uncomfortable with Uncertainty by Pema Chodron
Soul-Purpose by Mark Thurston
Path of Light by Robert Perry
The Untethered Soul by Michael A. Singer
365 Days of Walking the Red Road by Terri Jean
The Spirituality of Fasting by Charles M. Murphy
Don't Sweat the Small Stuff and It's All Small Stuff by Richard Carlson
The Light Inside by C.S. Drury
A Plain Account of Christian Perfection by John Wesley

~ ~ ~

Donna Fasano is a USA TODAY Bestselling author whose books have won awards and have sold nearly 4 million copies worldwide. Find her on the internet at DonnaFasano.com.

Cover design by Imogen Rose
ImogenRose.com

Photo Credits

Pages 14, 16, 18, and 26:
©Kristen Caudill, Kristen Caudill Photography
KristenCaudillPhotography.com
Permission granted for use via Kristen Caudill.

Pages 20, 22, and 24:
©Mishella, NY Classic Studios, Inc
NYClassicStudio.com
Permission granted for use via Getty Images (US), Inc.

Biblical references taken from the King James Version (KJV).

www.ingramcontent.com/pod-product-compliance
Lightning Source LLC
Chambersburg PA
CBHW041743040426
42444CB00001B/9